I0479743

Organizational Restructuring: Twelve Steps and Key Guidelines to help Business Managers

Zaziiz S. L. Dinkins, Th.D., D.B.A

WESTBOW
PRESS®
A DIVISION OF THOMAS NELSON
& ZONDERVAN

Copyright © 2022 Zaziiz S. L. Dinkins, Th.D., D.B.A.

All rights reserved. No part of this book may be used or reproduced by any means, graphic, electronic, or mechanical, including photocopying, recording, taping or by any information storage retrieval system without the written permission of the author except in the case of brief quotations embodied in critical articles and reviews.

WestBow Press books may be ordered through booksellers or by contacting:

WestBow Press
A Division of Thomas Nelson & Zondervan
1663 Liberty Drive
Bloomington, IN 47403
www.westbowpress.com
844-714-3454

Because of the dynamic nature of the Internet, any web addresses or links contained in this book may have changed since publication and may no longer be valid. The views expressed in this work are solely those of the author and do not necessarily reflect the views of the publisher, and the publisher hereby disclaims any responsibility for them.

Any people depicted in stock imagery provided by Getty Images are models, and such images are being used for illustrative purposes only. Certain stock imagery © Getty Images.

ISBN: 978-1-6642-6465-6 (sc)
ISBN: 978-1-6642-6464-9 (e)

Print information available on the last page.

WestBow Press rev. date: 5/5/2022

Dedication

This book is dedicated to all managers and leaders who may be considering organizational restructuring. I pray that in this book, you will find some insight or tip that will encourage you and help you to be successful at what you do. May God bless you!

Contents

Acknowledgments

I give praise, glory, and honor to God and my
Lord and Savior Jesus Christ for providing me
with knowledge, wisdom, understanding, skills
and guidance, and for establishing the work of
my hands. All glory to His name!

Foreword

To aid any organizational manager or leader in preparing for restructuring it is necessary to point out the targets of change while undertaking such a feat. It is also necessary to make clear the definition of organizational restructuring and to point out that the levels of change discussed here are interdependent, which suggests according to Matthew and Jones (2010) that it is very difficult to effect change at one level without effecting change at another level. Some of the key relevant questions to aid in the process of preparing for organizational restructuring are therefore discussed below for your information:

1. What is organizational restructuring?

It is a process used by managers to change assigned work and relationships with authority to redesign organizational structure and culture to improve organizational effectiveness (Jones & Matthew, 2010)

2. What does organizational restructuring do for organizations?

It targets the change of an organization at four levels of the organization.

3. **What are the four levels of an organization where change is targeted when the organization is going through the process of organizational restructuring?**

The four levels where change is targeted are: 1) The Human Resources Level, 2) The Functional Resources Level, 3) The Technological Capabilities Level, and 4) The Organizational Capabilities Level.

4. **What are the change efforts required at each of these four levels when going through the process of organizational restructuring?**

   a. The change efforts required at the Human Resources level are: 1) focus on a new investment in training and development activities so employees acquire new skills and abilities; 2) focus on socializing employees into the organizational culture so they learn the new routines on which the organizational performance depends; 3) focus on changing the organizational norms and values to motivate a cultural and diverse workforce; 4) focus on an on-going examination of the way in which the promotion and awards system operate in a diverse workforce; and 5) focus on changing the composition of the top management team to improve organizational learning and decision making (Jones & Matthew, 2010).

b. The change efforts required at the Functional Resources level are: 1) focus on the fact that each organizational function needs to develop procedures that allow it to manage the particular environment it faces; 2) focus on the fact that as the environment changes the organization needs to transfer resources to the function where the most values can be created; and 3) focus on improving the value that the organization's function created by changing the structure, culture, and technology (Jones & Matthew, 2010).

c. The change efforts required at the Technological Capabilities level are: 1) focus on developing a constant stream of new products to continue to attract customers; 2) focus on modifying existing products to continue to attract customers: 3) focus on improving the way goods and services are produced to increase their quality and reliability; and 4) focus on redesigning organizational activities to provide a context to translate technological competence into value for stakeholders (Jones & Matthew, 2010).

d. The change efforts required at the Organizational Capabilities level are: 1) focus on changing the relationships between people and functions to increase their ability to create value; 2) focus on changing the routines an individual uses to greet customers; 3) focus on changing workgroup relationships; 4) focus on improving the integration between divisions; and 5) focus on changing the corporate culture by changing the top management team (Jones & Matthew, 2010).

5. **What are the key factors that enable an organization's effectiveness and rapid growth?**

The key factors that enable an organization's effectiveness and rapid growth are: 1) control, 2) innovation, and 3) efficiency (Jones & Matthew, 2010).

6. **How do the key factors of control, innovation, and efficiency enable an organization's effectiveness and rapid growth?**

These factors are used to assess and measure how an organization creates value (Jones & Matthew, 2010).

7. **How does one assess and measure the organization's effectiveness in creating value?**

To assess and measure the organization's effectiveness in creating value it is imperative to: 1) focus on evaluating the organization's ability to secure, manage, and control scarce and valued skills and resources; 2) focus on evaluating the organization's ability to be innovative and to function quickly and responsibly; and 3) focus on evaluating the organization's ability to convert skills and resources into goods and services efficiently (Jones & Matthew, 2010).

I pray that these questions and answers will help to guide and keep you focus as you pursue the restructuring of your organization. I wish you all the best in your endeavors on this significant and important journey.

Zaziiz S. L. Dinkins, Th.D., D.B.A.

Introduction

Organizational Restructuring is a major change strategy commonly used to respond to changes in the business environment (Jones & Matthew, 2010; Bowman & Singh, 1993). It is "a process by which managers change task and authority relationships, and redesign organizational structure and culture to improve organizational effectiveness" (Jones & Matthew, 2010, p. 298). Organizational restructuring may be either internal, which includes technology upgrading, mergers, job layoffs, closing divisions or external, which includes asset disposal, acquisitions, divestures, start-ups, and closure of plants

(Bowman & Singh, 1993; Hakkala, 2006).). The focus here, nonetheless, is two-fold: (1) from an organizational restructuring perspective, it is about improving efficiency, reducing cost, and facilitating job growth (Fu, Chang, & Wu, 2001; Probst, 2003); (2) from an economic perspective, it is about the steps business executives can take to survive an economic down-turn.

It must be noted then, that "there have been 10 recognized U.S. recessions that covered approximately nine years in a nearly sixty-year period (1953, 1958, 1960-61, 1969-70, 1973-75, 1980, 1981-82, 1990-91, 2001, and 2007-2009)" (National Bureau of Economic Research, as cited in Byrd et al., 2012, p. 7). The succession of these recessions suggests that the United

States has been in a recession for one quarter of the 20th century, which does not appear to be unusual (Byrd et al., 2012). Not so long ago, regarding changes in U.S. job growth, President Obama, in the State of the Union address, specified that the economy needed to continue "churning out" high wage jobs (Fox News Videos, 2015). The president urged employers to do more to make Americans upgrade their skills and reward knowledge (Fox News Videos, 2015). President Obama specified that employers needed to provide more opportunity to workers so the workers could earn higher wage paying jobs, and that America had to put people back to work (Fox News Videos, 2015). President Obama also highlighted the fact that the United States did more than all economies combined, which in the end would impact the lives of families in a big way (Fox News Videos, 2015). Researchers such as Sharma, Garg, and Sharma (2011) have, therefore, concluded that even though the recession from 2007 to 2009, caused by the sub-prime mortgage crisis, lasted 18 months and affected the world's economy, the recession also provided an opportunity for some organizations to be innovative in finding ways to survive.

The following, therefore, reflects twelve steps business managers can take to help themselves in terms of organizational restructuring; and as you will note, these steps are indicative of the recommendations of a variety of subject matter experts on organizational restructuring and change. As you go through each step, take the time to make your own notes as to your own thoughts and opinion to help you navigate the way forward.

Step 1

Recognize what organizational restructuring entails

Organizational restructuring essentially concerns reducing cost, improving efficiency, and facilitating job growth (Fu et al., 2001; Probst, 2003). Organizational restructuring entails a reduction of one or more of the following: (a) an organization's overall size in terms of employees; (b) the number of units within an organization; (c) the size of the units within an organization; (d) the number of hierarchical levels within an organization, or rather, it could entail a reduction in a combination of all four areas (Keidel, 1994).

Emrich (2004) indicated that organizational restructuring entails a plan for job creation, expansion, retention, and attraction. And Meckstroth (1993) declared that the key factor in the job expansion was a long-term growth strategy, which encompassed increasing saving and investment. Meckstroth (1993) further indicated that sustaining an expansion required new sources of capital in the form of income and earnings that could only derive from the creation of new jobs.

Rogers and Doty (2010) expressed how the job retention and expansion entailed local entrepreneurs who increased their product lines, kept and created jobs, grew their investments, how they took advantage of opportunities, and diversified their product lines to increase their competitiveness. Rogers and Doty (2010) specified how entrepreneurs also formed partnerships with companies that had retention and expansion projects, which created capital for private investments (Rogers & Doty, 2010). The entrepreneurial partnerships created a momentum, which resulted in an increase of manufacturing activities, business expansion, and significant growth in investments. Rogers and Doty (2010) further pointed out how entrepreneurs analyzed and researched various industries and how they took advantage of slow job growth and diversified their economic base by leveraging from several different market positions. The strategies that were utilized by entrepreneurial partners encouraged community and business development, attracted new businesses, and raised awareness for job creation and job growth (Rogers & Doty, 2010).

Restructuring essentially then provides an organization with a competitive strategy for the development of key resources and capabilities (Jones, 2006). It invokes a balance of power that must be sustained by top management both internally and externally (Soulsby & Clark, 2013).

Notes

Step 2

Understand the impact of organizational restructuring

Reifman (1995) specified that the impact of restructuring on jobs was that there were more productivity and greater earnings with lesser employees. Hakkala (2006) also commented on the impact and stated that labor productivity increase was reflective of production as well as technological change and was highly concentrated on skills.

Notes

Step 3

Recognize the role of the key factors of organizational restructuring

The key factors of organizational restructuring include control, innovation, and efficiency (Jones & Matthew, 2010). Managers use the three processes to measure and determine their effectiveness in creating value for their organization and in establishing a competitive edge (Jones & Matthew, 2010).

The first factor, control, relates to the ability of an organization to acquire effectively scarce and valued resources and skills (Jones & Matthew, 2010). Control is a process by which managers exercise influence over their external organizational environment and at the same time attract resources and customers (Jones & Matthew, 2010). The ability to influence key stakeholder is crucial to the survival of the organization. As a result, managers utilize effective measurement tools such as the return on investment, stock pricing, and profitability to exercise control over their environment. These measurement tools provide CEOs with an advantage to take hold of the new market opportunities, and to be able to respond to changes as they occur, in a timely and efficient manner (Jones & Matthew, 2010). Their willingness to pursue the development of new products and services that takes advantage of market conditions, and their competitive attitude is what set them apart and determine how well they control the organization's environment (Jones & Matthew, 2010).

The control of an organization's environment is also concerned with the integration of the employees' and the organization's actions that fulfill shared goals and intentions (Bredmar, 2011). The process creates meaning for the organization (Bredmar, 2011). Organizations with management control systems are in the best interest of organizations because having such systems in place increase the probability that the employees will make decisions that are on behalf of the organization (Bredmar, 2011).

The second factor, innovation, relates to the ability of an organization to operate and function effectively and to be innovative and quickly responsive (Jones & Matthew, 2010). Innovation allows the organization to be flexible in making decisions and to be creative in producing new products and services in a rapid manner (Jones & Matthew, 2010). Managers use innovation as a process within the organization to introduce new structures and cultures to the organization and to develop its skills and capabilities so that the organization does not only change, adapt, and improve its functionality, but also learn of new products and processes (Jones & Matthew, 2010).

Innovation also entails creativity, which is very significant to the organization when establishing a competitive advantage (Beheshtifar & Kamani-Fard, 2013). The creativity of the organization encompasses removing barriers, managing innovation, evaluating ideas, motivating and stimulating communication, developing the sources of ideas and the creative planning process, and working with others in a complex social system (Beheshtifar & Kamani-Fard, 2013). The resources necessary for innovation includes those made available to employees in terms of finance, material, information; training for the improvement of creative thinking skills; and the time provided for creative thinking and the exploration of accomplishing new tasks (Beheshtifar & Kamani-Fard, 2013).

The third factor, efficiency, relates to the ability of organizational managers to change resources and skills into products and services (Jones & Matthew, 2010). Efficiency is a process by which managers develop production facilities by utilizing futuristic technologies and techniques to produce, distribute, and improve an organization's product in a manner that is both timely, and cost effective (Jones & Matthew, 2010). Organizational leaders who use efficiency strategies build the organization's culture (Su, Yang, & Yang, 2012), which is the foundation of structural stability within the organization (Schein, 2010). However, the use of efficiency strategies all depends on a match between strategies (Su et al., 2012). For example, strategies used in manufacturing and building organizational culture do not coincide with each other and cause inefficiency in production and competition within the organization (Su et al., 2012). Strategies that coincide in both areas produce a competitive advantage and excellent performance (Su et al., 2012).

Notes

Step 4

Recognize the basis of the organization's improvement programs and goals

Findings relating to successful restructuring improvement programs revealed certain common characteristics (Tichy & Nisberg, 1976). The first characteristic is the explicit and purposeful program goals and directions (Tichy & Nisberg, 1976). The second characteristic is that the organization of the program and its resources are allocated based on task requirements and not on authority and power (Tichy & Nisberg, 1976). The third characteristic is the location of information, and not the roles in hierarchy, which determines where decisions are made, and the problems are resolved when the expert resources are brought together (Tichy & Nisberg, 1976). And the final and fourth characteristic is the organizational innovation, design, and the close attention of management to the organizational context (Tichy & Nisberg, 1976).

Notes

Step 5

Get a clear understanding of the organization's current structure

Bolman and Deal (2013) were very specific when they highlighted factors for success. According to Bolman and Deal (2013), one of the key factors for success in organizational restructuring was getting a clear understanding of the current structure of the organization process. Bolman and Deal (2013) indicated that it is very important to understand what worked and what did not work in the process.

Notes

_____

_____

_____

_____

_____

_____

_____

_____

_____

_____

_____

_____

_____

_____

Step 6

Recognize the role of the organization's employees, middle managers, and Chief Executive Officers in terms of leadership and management

The organization's design and change are as important at the frontline supervisory level as they are at the CEO level because executive managers as well as lower-level employees are affected in terms of restructuring efforts (Jones & Matthew, 2010; NELP, 2014; Probst, 2003). Restructuring is a major process that takes time and resources (Bolman & Deal, 2013).

When organizational leaders restructure, there is no guarantee that the process will succeed (Bolman & Deal, 2013). As a result, managers of organizations must consider the differences in structural configuration and their competing interests (Bolman & Deal, 2013). Top executive managers are the key players in the restructuring process because they are mainly responsible for the negotiating of the organization's new structure (Bolman & Deal, 2013). Restructuring decisions then play a key role in strategic planning, and the consequences involve stakeholders, performance, and a competitive edge (Bowman & Singh, 1993).

Panic (2012) commented on organizational restructuring and two of its important aspects and indicated that stability, ethics, and honesty were motivational factors that produced dedication, customer care, and innovation in an organization's employees and that justice and communication were the two most important aspects of organizational restructuring. Balogun's (2007) position on organizational restructuring and practice pointed out the significant role middle managers played in organizational restructuring because middle managers were the ones usually tasked with working the plans of senior management.

Organizational restructuring requires senior managers to be fully aware of the challenges facing the organization because during the period of change, system development as well as standardization and uniformity become crucial (Alvi et al., 2013).

It should also be noted that not all organizational leaders are able to make a transformation when facing the challenges of a changing environment (Dervitsiotis, 2013). For example, change in terms of technology may cause the organization to decline or even disappear; and to control the restructuring process managers must face a powerful opposition that exists among other senior managers as well as stakeholders (Dervitsiotis, 2013).

Additionally, even though restructuring an organization to adjust successfully to environmental changes is a complex process

(Panic, 2012), the management team of an organization is comprised of department managers, senior managers, and employees who want to act in meaningful ways, and who keep constant dialogue between them (Bredmar, 2011). The management team members increase the probability that they will make decisions and take actions that are in the organization's best interest and point to the many influences on the organization (Bredmar, 2011).

The main concern then becomes the development of leadership and management skills, and the upgrade team building, motivational, performance, and change management skills (Alvi et al., 2013). While developing such a system becomes vital, standardization is of concern (Alvi et al., 2013). The CEO must take initiatives to erase any differences between strategy and implementation by making sure that the communication and coordination in the system flows smoothly (Alvi et al., 2013).

Notes

Step 7

Make the right connection between business process re-engineering and organizational restructuring

Restructuring relates closely to re-engineering because in practice, changing an organization's structure to a more efficient one usually causes employee layoffs (Jones & Matthew, 2010). However, if the organization has sufficient growth, the leaders may be able to transfer employees in other areas of the organization (Jones & Matthew, 2010). So, while re-engineering in terms of the business process mainly concerns how a product is produced, organizational restructuring, in contrast, concerns the issues of authority and control and the appropriateness of the levels and functions of departments in the hierarchy of an organization (Chen & Tsai, 2008).

Notes

_____

_____

_____

_____

_____

_____

_____

_____

_____

_____

_____

_____

_____

_____

Step 8

Develop new ideas

According to Bolman and Deal (2013), it is very important to develop new ideas of the organization's objectives and goals. This contributes to the overall success of the organization's restructuring. It is also very important for the senior managers to consider why the organization needs restructuring and to view the situation in an opposite light by asking "What is wrong today?" (Recardo & Heather,

2013). This can help leaders and managers to envision what they want the organization to be like tomorrow and thereby help them to develop new ideas.

Notes

_____

_____

_____

_____

_____

_____

_____

_____

_____

_____

_____

_____

_____

_____

Step 9

Design a new structure

Bowman and Singh (1993) specified, "Organizational restructuring is intended to increase the efficiency and effectiveness of management teams through significant changes in organizational structure, often accompanied by downsizing" (p. 6). The downsizing, which is about reducing costs, may seem contrary to popular belief or opinion. Keidel (1994) indicated, however, "The overriding performance criterion is efficiency" (p. 13), which makes possible a successful future for the organization from an economic perspective. It is, therefore, important to design a new structure that responds to the changes facing the organization in terms of goals and objectives, technology, and the external and internal environment.

Notes

Step 10

Align the organization's structure with its environment and technology

The managers of the organization must ensure that the organization's structure aligns with its environment and its technology (Bolman & Deal, 2013). In other words, the managers must ensure that the organization's strategies are in alignment with the situations facing the organization. Jones (2006) discussed organizational restructuring and globalization and indicated that the restructuring of any type should be very clear and specifically in alignment with the business strategy of an organization in order to effectively and efficiently allocate resources at a maximum and to attain a competitive advantage.

Notes

_____

_____

_____

_____

_____

_____

_____

_____

_____

_____

_____

_____

_____

_____

_____

Step 11

Launch the right strategy

Tram and Vandenbosch (1998) indicated that successful organizational restructuring depended on launching the right strategy. The right restructuring strategy is important because it amounts to choosing the best strategy that will enhance the company's value (Tram & Vandenbosch, 1998). Middle managers are, therefore, significant in the role they play in restructuring because they are the ones who implement the plans of senior management (Balogun, 2007). Consequently, senior managers must ensure that there are no disconnections between strategy and implementation (Alvi et al., 2013). Senior managers are ultimately responsible to develop a lasting and holistic plan that is in alignment with the organization's culture and strategy (Alvi et al., 2013).

And so while the response to an economic downturn is usually a reduction in staff due to less revenue, there are many strategies that employers use to cut costs, eliminate waste, and maintain morale and productivity (Byrd, Smith & Helms, 2012). Some of the strategies employers can use include "delaying expansions, deferring maintenance and special projects; freezing training, business travel, and non-essential spending for supplies and services; and decreasing expenses" (Byrd et al., 2012, p. 6).

Another strategic response to the pressure and the effects of restructuring, which involves the workplace, is organizational flexibility (Kalleberg, 2003). According to Kalleberg (2003), organizational flexibility could make a significant difference in the outcome of the restructuring. Kalleberg (2003) specified that there were two forms of organizational flexibility: functional flexibility, which is internal, and numerical flexibility, which is external.

Kalleberg (2003) indicated that functional flexibility was the ability of an organization to redeploy a worker from one task to another. In other words, the workers are empowered to take part in decision making, participate in various teams, and recommit themselves to the organization. The workers can link their compensation to the performance of the organization, which researchers referred to as "high performance work" (Kalleberg, 2003, p. 154). Numerical flexibility entails the organization's manipulation of the size of the organization's workforce in concert with demanding fluctuations by utilizing workers that are not full-time, or by requiring the full-time employees to work overtime. Kalleberg (2003) stated that the external workforce was comprised of several kinds of non-standard work relations. Kalleberg (2003) pointed out that employment could be limited using part-time or short-term temporary workers who can be hired and released quickly, were utilized when there were no authorizations to hire, and which cost less than the full-time employees did. Kalleberg (2003) stated when the temporary workers were on the payroll, they did not have strong ties with the organization, received very few benefits, and worked on an as-needed basis.

One can also look at the best practices for example in terms of downsizing. Cameron (1994) shared the following three approaches:

- Use a long-term strategy instead of focusing on one program that may be abandoned or disappear once it completed.

- Develop and invest in the ideas of the organization's human resources.

- Seek to continuously improve as opposed to operating in a continuous mode of crisis. (pp. 207-208)

Leaders must be able to envision how the organization's restructuring program will be of support to its competitive strategy and determine the tactical measures and strategic adjustments of the organization's boundaries both internally and externally to stakeholders (Jones, 2006).

Notes

Step 12

———•⧴≋⧳•———

Be flexible and experiment

According to Bolman and Deal (2013), it is very important to be flexible and to dare to experiment. As the organization responds to changes, keep the things that work and remove the things that do not work (Bolman & Deal, 2013).

In terms of organizational restructuring, it must be noted that company leaders who restructure successfully develop a sound strategy that includes a fresh mindset. They have an early warning system to scan the environment. They assess their freedom to act, and they utilize a holistic approach to balance competition for investment, resources, and customers (Block, 2001; Tram & Vandenbosch, 1998). Successful organizational restructuring requires continuous learning and a willingness to change (Fu et al., 2001). The process involves "employee involvement, teamwork, communication and information sharing, rewarding, appraising, training, articulating a vision, and administering downsizing in a trustworthy and fair manner" (Cameron, 1994, p. 210). The restructuring process in essence encompasses an approach to human resource as an asset instead of a liability, an approach that is a long-term strategy as well as one that is viewed as an opportunity for improvement (Cameron, 1994).

Notes

Key Guidelines for Organizational Restructuring

In addition to the previous Twelve Steps, to help you restructure your organization, here are some key guidelines you should also focus on, and adhere to, on this significant journey (Recardo & Heather, 2013):

1. **Ensure you have the support of your Top Management.** Start out with the support and sponsorship of Senior Management and other organizational leaders (internal and external) that impact the organization being restructured. This means that the key

decision makers will agree that a change is required and therefore will agree on the timing and the competing initiatives, and that they will agree to develop and validate the strategy that will drive the restructuring.

2. **Ensure you connect strategy to the design of the organization.** Connecting strategy to design will bring about a more holistic answer to the organizational issues that needs to be addressed. It doesn't matter what the vision and mission of the organization is, the strategy adopted should significantly influence the way the organization is designed or organized. This includes internal factors such as customers, competitors, supplies, employee culture, as well as external factors

such as the economy, politics, industry, social trends, the environment, and government.

3. **Ensure you use a well-structured approach as you embark on this journey.** It is most important to use a process that is reliable, data-driven, transparent, and repeatable in conjunction with clear communication which involves 3 phases. Phase 1 – You must define. This means you will organize the project, establish the design parameters, and assess the current state. Phase 2 – You must design. This means you will address the macro design; the detailed design and you will benchmark against the best in the industry. Phase 3 – You must implement. This means you will conduct a pilot test

to ensure the functionality of the new design. Once approved, you put the new design into operation. It is also imperative that you address all the people and change management issues. This includes the stakeholders, candidates to fill key and vacant positions, competency, gap and other project related issues.

4. **Ensure the business process work is kept very simple.** This means that the organization's design will be driven by business strategy and not by the organization's processes. The first question to ask is: what kind of work the organization should be doing, which will be linked with execution. The link with strategy can

be divided into operating processes and management processes. Whereas the link with execution will estimate how much time key resources will have to spend on process analysis and design work.

5. **Ensure you collect and use all your data.** Collect data from appropriate stakeholders, internal and external, with similar structures to understand customer requirements, strengths, weaknesses and performance gaps to help with suggestions for improvement and various ways of structuring.

6. **Ensure you consider your various options.** Organizational restructuring is not a "one

size fits all" project. To move quickly, some steps in the restructuring process can be skipped but to ensure sound business decisions it is essential to stick to some core steps.

7. **Ensure you are aware of all the trade-offs.** In other words, leaders must carefully pick their battles. Senior leaders need to think past the implementation so they can clearly understand where the direction of the new design will take them. Try to list as many negative aspects of the design as positives

which, in turn, will lead to good decision making.

8. **Ensure you keep the focus on the people.** People are our most important resource. Internal as well as external stakeholders need help to adjust to changes brought on by restructuring. Therefore, look into change management at the start of the project rather than at the end. Leaders must identify the effects of restructuring on its people and practices as well as the change management issues involved.

9. **Ensure you do not declare victory too early.** Set up various methods of coordination so

that units work together effectively. Identify sources and causes of problem. Understand how processes are linked. Develop Standard Operating Procedures, policies, practices, and appoint managers to oversee the different units.

10. **Ensure you are on top of the IT Systems.** Ensure there is someone included from IT on the restructuring project. Knowing the functional strengths and pitfalls of technology associated with the organization

under restructuring is critical to the design decision.

I wish you good luck with your Organizational Restructuring project, and all the best to you in all your future endeavors.

Dr. Z. S. L. Dinkins, Th.D., D.B.A.

References

Alvi, S., Butt, A. N., & Khurshid, A. (2013). Beaconhouse School System (BSS) restructuring. *Asian Journal of Management Cases, 10*(22), 113-124. doi:10.1177/0972820113493687

Balogun, J. (2007). The practice of organizational restructuring: From design to reality. *European Management journal, 25*(2), 81-91. doi:10.1016/j.emj.2007.02.001

Beheshtifar, M., & Kamani-Fard, F. B. (2013). Organizational creativity: A substantial factor to growth. *International Journal of*

Academic Research in Business and Social Sciences, 3(3), 98-104. Retrieved from http://journalseeker.researchbib.com

Block, L. (2001). Perspectives on organizational change. *Futurics, 25*(3/4), 67-87. Retrieved from http://www.journals.elsevier.com/futures/

Bolman, L. G., & Deal, T. E. (2013). *Reframing organizations: Artistry, choice, and leadership* (5th ed.). San Francisco, CA: Jossey-Bass.

Bowman, E. H., & Singh, H. (1993). Corporate restructuring: Reconfiguring the firm. *Strategic Management Journal, 14,* 5-14. Retrieved from http://onlinelibrary.wiley.com/journal

Bredmar, K. (2011). Management control: A process that creates organizational meaning. *Global Business and Management Research: An International Journal, 3*(2), 106-118. Retrieved from http://gbmr.ioksp.com/archives.htm

Byrd, J., Smith, D., & Helms, M. M. (2012). How to prosper during an economic downturn. *The CPA Journal.* Retrieved from http://nysscpa.org/cpaj.htm

Cameron, K. S. (1994). Strategies for successful organizational downsizing. *Human Resource Management, 33*(2), 189-211. doi:10.1002/hrm.3930330204

Chen, C. K., & Tsai, C. H. (2008). Developing a process re-engineering-oriented organizational change exploratory simulation system (PROCESS). *International Journal of Production Research, 46*(16), 4463-4482. doi:10.1080/ 00207540601182286.

Dervitsiotis, K. N. (2003). The pursuit of sustainable business excellence: Guiding transformation for effective organizational change. *Total Quality Management, 14*(3), 251-267. doi:10.1080/1478336032000046599

Emrich, A. B. (2004). Restructuring needed for future job growth. *Grand Rapids Business Journal.* Retrieved from http://grbj.com

Fox News (Producer) (2015). State of the Union Address (Video). Available from http://news. yahoo.com/photos/obama-economy

Fu, H. P., Chang, T. H., & Wu, M. J. (2001). A case study of the SMEs' organizational restructuring in Taiwan. *Industrial Management and Data System, 101*(8/9). Retrieved from http://www. emeraldgrouppublishing.com

Hakkala, K. (2006). Corporate restructuring and labor productivity growth. *Industrial and Corporate Change, 15*(4), 683-714. doi:10.1093/icc/dt1015

Jones, G. R., & Matthew, M. (2010). *Organizational theory, design, and change*

(6th ed.). Upper Saddle River, NJ: Prentice Hall.

Jones, M. T. (2006). Globalization and organizational restructuring: A strategic perspective. *Thunderbird International Business Review, 44*(3), 325-351. Retrieved from http://onlinelibrary.wiley.com/ journal/10.1002

Kalleberg, A. L. (2003). Flexible firms and labor market segmentation: Effects of workplace restructuring on jobs and workers. *Work and Occupations, 30*(2), 154-175. doi:10.1177/0730888403251683.

Kanten, S., & Yaslioglu, M. (2012). Role of innovation in creating customer value in hotel establishments: A study on managers. *The Journal of Faculty of Economics and Administrative Sciences, 17*(2), 437-449. Retrieved from http://iibfdergi.sdu.edu.tr/en

Keidel, R. (1994). Rethinking organizational design. *The Academy of Management Executive, 8*(4). Retrieved from http://www.sil.si.edu/eresources/silpurl.cfm?purl=1079-5545

Meckstroth, D. J. (1993). The missing ingredient in the economic expansion-new jobs. *Business Economics, 28*(3), 29-24. Retrieved from http://www.palgrave-journals.com/be/index.html

National Employment Law Project [NELP]. (2014). *Tracking the low-wage recovery: Industry employment and wages.* Retrieved from www.nelp.org

Panic, S. (2012). Responsible restructuring the most important aspects. *Management Journal for Theory and Practice Management, 63,* 85-89. doi:10.7595/ management.fon.2012.0016

Probst, T. M. (2003). Exploring employee outcomes of organizational restructuring: A Solomon four-group study. *Group and Organizational Management, 28*(3), 416-439. doi:10.1177/1059601102250825

Recardo, R. J., & Heather, K. (2013). Ten Best Practices for Restructuring the Organization.

Global Business and Organizational Excellence, 23-37. doi:10.1002/joe.21470

Reifman, S. Z. (1995). Jobs and productivity. *The Forbes 500s,* 254-274. Retrieved from http://www.forbes.com

Rogers, T. G., & Doty, R. L. (2010). Richmond forecast 2011. *Indiana Business Review, 85*(4), 39-40. Retrieved from http://www. ibrc.indiana.edu/ibr/

Schein, E. H. (2010). *Organizational culture and leadership* (4th ed.). San Francisco, CA: Jossey-Bass.

Sharma, D., Garg, S. K., & Sharma, C. (2011). Strategies for SMEs after global recession. *Global Business and Management Research,*

3(1), 58-60. Retrieved from http://www.gbmr.ioksp.com/

Soulsby, A., & Clark, E. (2013). Organizational restructuring and change in transition societies: Dominant coalitions and the dynamic of managerial power and politics. *Competition and Change, 17*(2), 176-196. doi:10.1179/1024529413Z. 00000000032

Su, Z., Yang, D., & Yang, J. (2012). The match between efficiency/flexibility strategy and organizational culture. *International Journal of Production Research, 50*(19), 5317-5329. Retrieved from http://www.scimagojr.com

Tichy, N. M., & Nisberg, J. N. (1976). When does restructuring work? Organizational

innovations at Volvo and GM. *Organizational*
Dynamics, 5(1), 63-80. Retrieved from
http://www.journals.elsevier.com/
organizationaldynamics/

Tram, M. R., & Vandenbosch, M. (1998).
Restructuring: Making it work. *Strategy*
and Leadership, 26(3), 24-28. Retrieved from
http://www.emeraldinsight.com/loi/sl

www.ingramcontent.com/pod-product-compliance
Lightning Source LLC
Chambersburg PA
CBHW021451210526
45463CB00002B/738